W9-APM-755

FAR-OUT GUIDE TO

EARTH

Mary Kay Carson

Bailey Books
an imprint of
Enslow Publishers, Inc.
40 Industrial Road
Box 398
Berkeley Heights, NJ 07922
USA
http://www.enslow.com

For Megan Hanna Barb

Bailey Books, an imprint of Enslow Publishers, Inc.

Copyright © 2011 by Mary Kay Carson

All rights reserved.

No part of this book may be reproduced by any means
without the written permission of the publisher.

Library of Congress Cataloging-in-Publication Data

Carson, Mary Kay.
    Far-out guide to Earth / Mary Kay Carson.
        p. cm. — (Far-out guide to the solar system)
    Summary: "Presents information about Earth, including fast facts, history, and technology used to study
the planet"—Provided by publisher.
    Includes bibliographical references and index.
    ISBN 978-0-7660-3182-1 (Library Ed.)
    ISBN 978-1-59845-183-2 (Paperback Ed.)
    1. Earth—Juvenile literature. 2. Solar system—Juvenile literature. I. Title.
QB631.4.C37 2011
525—dc22
                                   2008049781

Printed in China

052010 Leo Paper Group, Heshan City, Guangdong, China

10 9 8 7 6 5 4 3 2 1

To Our Readers: We have done our best to make sure all Internet addresses in this book were active and appropriate when we went to press. However, the author and the publisher have no control over and assume no liability for the material available on those Internet sites or on other Web sites they may link to. Any comments or suggestions can be sent by e-mail to comments@enslow.com or to the address on the back cover.

Image Credits: Acme Design Company, p. 37; FWS/Elizabeth Labunski, p. 42; Lunar and Planetary Institute, p. 26; NASA, pp. 9, 10, 13, 15, 16, 23, 38, 40; NASA/Goddard Space Flight Center Scientific Visualization Studio, pp. 3, 18, 28, 39; NASA/JPL, pp. 4–5; NASA/Visible Earth, pp. 1, 24; NPS Photo by Jim Peaco, p. 12; Tom Uhlman/ www.tomuphoto.com, pp. 6, 7, 27 (mountains), 30, 31, 35; USGS, p. 27 (volcano).

Cover Image: NASA/Visible Earth

CONTENTS

INTRODUCTION
5

CHAPTER 1
ZOOMING IN ON EARTH
9

EARTH AT A GLANCE
18

FAST FACTS ABOUT EARTH
19

EARTH TIMELINE OF
EXPLORATION AND DISCOVERY
22

CHAPTER 2
EARTH AS A PLANET
25

CHAPTER 3
WHAT'S NEXT FOR EARTH?
34

WORDS TO KNOW
44

FIND OUT MORE AND GET UPDATES
46

INDEX
48

Earth

EARTH is the third planet from the Sun. *(Note that the planets' distances are not shown to scale.)*

INTRODUCTION

Did you know that Earth's day is getting longer? The day grows longer by about one to two thousandths of a second about every hundred years. What's causing our days to stretch? Earth's spin is slowing. One spin is one day, so a slower spin makes a day last longer. How do we know this? Scientists use atomic clocks to compare the time to day length. You will learn lots more far-out facts about Earth in this book. Just keep reading!

Earth is the fifth largest planet in our solar system and the third closest to the Sun. But Earth is first when we talk about life. It is the only known place where life thrives. The more we explore and learn about other planets, the more we realize how special Earth is.

FAR-OUT FACT

SYSTEM OF SPHERES

Earth is a system made up of different parts, called spheres. The outermost sphere is the atmosphere. This is Earth's air. Then there is the watery hydrosphere. It is the layer of ocean, rivers, lakes, and ice sheets that covers much of Earth's surface. The lithosphere is made of rocks, land, and underground earth. The biosphere is the living layer. It is where Earth's life-forms live within the other spheres.

Earth's distance from the Sun makes it the right temperature for liquid water—something all known forms of life need. Earth's neighbor Venus is closer to the Sun. It has a thicker layer of air than Earth. This makes it so hot that its water boiled away long ago. Earth's other neighbor, Mars, is chilly. It has little air and is farther away from the Sun than Earth. Its water is frozen.

Earth's size helps make it livable, too. Our planet is big enough to have the gravity needed to hold onto its layer of surrounding air, or atmosphere. Much of the air around smaller worlds floated off into space long ago. An atmosphere gives living things air to breathe. It also blocks the Sun's harmful rays.

EARTH is the only known place where life swims, hops, sprouts, runs, flies, and grows.

EARTH SYSTEM SCIENCE

Earth's unique environment is possible because of our planet's air, water, rocks, and life. Earth is a system created by these combined parts working together. Each part affects the others. For example, pollution in the air can mix with rain. When the rain fills up streams, it becomes water pollution. Life—especially human life— also affects Earth. People have made Earth a different planet than it was centuries ago. The world population has doubled since the 1950s. Earth's environment is changing as people fill up its land and use up its forests, water, minerals, and other resources.

Scientists studying Earth are tracking these changes. They are measuring air and water pollution, studying weather and storms, and watching how well different plants and animals are surviving. Scientists want to know how these changes are affecting our planet. Are they upsetting Earth's balance? Can the planet's complex system continue without problems? The answers they find will affect us all.

CHAPTER 1

ZOOMING IN ON EARTH

Sometimes a different view really changes how you see something. Think of looking at a rock with a magnifier. You may see tiny mineral grains or other details. Now imagine zooming out and seeing our rocky world from space. People shrink and streets disappear. Mountains become bumps on chunks of land surrounded by lots of blue ocean water.

THE *Apollo 8* astronauts were the first humans to see Earth from deep space in 1968.

The *Apollo 8* astronauts were the first people to see Earth like this. The astronauts were on their way to orbit the Moon in 1968. They looked back at Earth in awe—and took photographs. Seeing our planet alone against the darkness of space changed the way many humans viewed it. People saw Earth as a whole— one system with shared air, land, water, and life.

A VIEW FROM SPACE

Apollo 8's mission was during a decade when scientists were chasing the dream of landing astronauts on the Moon. (They succeeded in 1969 with *Apollo 11*.) But some scientists had a different dream. They wanted to use space technology to look at our own planet. A view from space makes it possible to track changes all around the globe. The secret to getting that view is satellites.

A satellite is a machine launched into space that circles Earth. The first satellite went into Earth orbit in 1957. Today, nearly 3,000 satellites

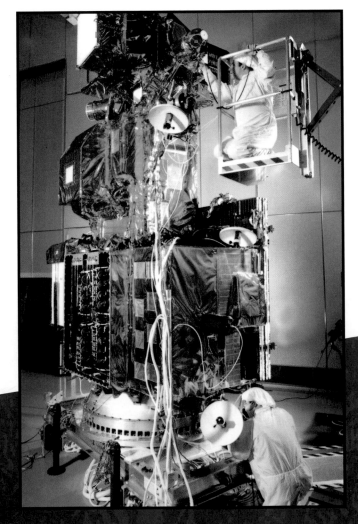

ENGINEERS work on *Landsat 7* before launch. The satellite went into orbit around Earth on April 15, 1999.

RACING TO GET SATELLITES INTO SPACE

In 1955, two nations announced plans to be the first to launch a satellite. The Soviet Union and the United States both competed in the space race to prove that their form of government was superior. And both nations wanted spy satellites capable of looking in on their enemies—each other. The United States lost the space race. The Soviet Union successfully launched *Sputnik* in October 1957. The United States launched its first satellite, *Explorer I*, about four months later. It was not a friendly competition. Satellites have a less than peaceful past! But they have become a powerful tool for scientists.

circle our planet. They help us predict weather, make phone calls, watch television, guide airplanes and ships, and spy on enemies. Satellites are also amazing tools for Earth scientists. Taking pictures from up above is the best way to keep track of shrinking forests, melting ice caps, or growing deserts.

GETTING THE BIG PICTURE

Landsat was the first Earth-studying satellite program. This system of satellites takes pictures of Earth's land.

FAR-OUT FACT

HOW LANDSAT HELPS BISON

During winter, some of the bison in Yellowstone National Park wander out of the park in search of grass to eat. The animals are caught and returned to the park. However, deciding where and when to let them go can be tricky. If they are set free where deep snow will bury the grass for weeks to come, the bison will just leave the park again. The Landsat program is helping by mapping snow depths daily throughout the park. Wildlife scientists use the maps to choose the least snowy areas to set bison loose.

THESE Landsat images show the same area of forest in Papua New Guinea in 1990 (left) and 2001 (below). Notice the new farms and roads that have replaced forests.

Landsat 1 was launched atop a rocket in 1972 and started sending back never-before-seen views from 900 kilometers (560 miles) above Earth.

Nearly forty years and six Landsat satellites later, we now have millions of images of Earth over time. Landsat satellites have taken pictures of volcanoes erupting, mountains moving, wildfires burning, glaciers melting, and coastlines changing. Landsat images are like a collection of family photo albums of Earth.

A POWERFUL VIEW

People and governments around the world—scientists, foresters, farmers, business owners, and engineers—want Landsat pictures. Terry Arvidson has been a part of Landsat's program for almost thirty years. Arvidson's job is to help make sure the latest satellite, *Landsat 7*, delivers. "After launch in 1999, all the folks who helped build the satellite headed off to other programs," Arvidson explained. "[I]f anything goes wrong on the satellite, I get in touch with them . . . to help . . . solve the problem."

Landsat 7 is a powerful tool for studying our planet. It orbits 705 kilometers (438 miles) above Earth, nearly twice as high as the International Space Station. But its instruments can see things on Earth as small as a house. Every ninety-nine minutes, *Landsat 7* makes a complete loop around our planet. It only takes sixteen days for it to take images of all Earth's land.

MAKING A DIFFERENCE

Landsat pictures help all sorts of scientists study Earth. They help weather scientists track snow cover from year to year. They can see widespread disasters like floods, hurricanes, and tornadoes. Landsat pictures show where

THESE are Landsat images of a California wildfire in 2006. The true-color image (top) shows the smoke plumes while the heat image (right) shows where flames are burning. Landsat pictures help firefighters zero in on big wildfires.

DUBAI is one of the world's fastest-growing cities. Landsat images of the city from 1973 (left) and 2006 (right) show more roads and buildings, as well as a constructed harbor and two artificial islands shaped like palm trees.

forests are shrinking and deserts are growing. They track sprawling cities and lakes that are drying up. Terry Arvidson understands how important Landsat pictures are for keeping track of our changing planet. She likes "working on a project that benefits mankind, that's going to help us understand what we're doing to planet Earth and how we need to change in order to preserve Earth for future generations."

Landsat satellites send their information to ground stations around the globe. So Arvidson gets to travel and make friends in other countries. That is another part of the job she likes. Arvidson's passions are to travel and to help preserve this planet for future generations. She can do that with Landsat!

FAR-OUT FACT

LANDSAT 8

Both *Landsat 5* and *Landsat 7* continue to orbit Earth and send back pictures today. But they will not last forever. The Landsat satellites are the longest continuous record of Earth's surface. No one wants the pictures to stop coming in, so another Landsat satellite is in the works. *Landsat 8*, the Landsat Data Continuity Mission (LDCM), is set to launch in late 2012. *Landsat 8* will be able to scan 66 percent more of Earth per day than *Landsat 7*.

EARTH AT A GLANCE

Diameter: 12,756 kilometers (7,926 miles)

Volume: 1,083,200,000,000 kilometers^3 (259,900,000,000 miles^3)

Mass: 5,973,700,000,000 trillion kilograms

Speed Around Sun: 107,229 kilometers (66,629 miles) per hour

Position: Third planet from the Sun

Average Distance from Sun: 149,597,890 kilometers (92,955,820 miles)

Day Length: 24 hours

Year Length: 365 ¼ Earth days

Color: Blue

Atmosphere: 77 percent nitrogen, 21 percent oxygen, 2 percent other gases

Surface: Water and rock

Minimum/Maximum Surface Temperature: –88/58 degrees Celsius (–126/136 degrees Fahrenheit)

Moons: 1

Rings: None

Symbol:

EARTH

Planet Fast Facts

★ Earth is the fifth largest planet in the solar system.

★ Earth is the largest of our solar system's four solid, rocky planets (Mercury, Venus, Earth, and Mars).

★ Its distance from the Sun and its atmosphere create Earth's life-supporting temperatures.

★ Earth's center, or core, is liquid iron and nickel metal. The core's temperature is hotter than the surface of the Sun.

★ Earth's fast spin and metal core create a magnetic field around the planet.

★ Earth spins at a tilt so different places get more focused sunlight during parts of the year, creating seasons.

★ One large moon orbits Earth. Earth's moon is the largest in the solar system compared to the size of its planet.

★ Earth is the only one of the eight planets whose name does not come from Greek or Roman mythology. Our planet has many names in many languages. "Earth" comes from an Old English word.

Air Fast Facts

★ The blanket of air surrounding Earth is called the atmosphere.

★ Earth's atmosphere is mostly nitrogen (77 percent) and oxygen (21 percent) with small amounts of other gases, including carbon dioxide, argon, and water vapor.

★ The blue color of the sky is caused by Earth's sunlight-scattering atmosphere that lets blue light through.

★ Earth's atmosphere provides animals and people with air to breathe, as well as protection from harmful rays of the Sun and from most meteors, which burn up before hitting the planet's surface.

★ Without life there would be no oxygen in Earth's air; it comes from plants during photosynthesis.

Water Fast Facts

★ The hydrosphere is the watery oceans, rivers, lakes, and ice sheets that cover much of Earth's surface.

★ Nearly 70 percent of Earth is covered in ocean at least 4 kilometers (2.5 miles) deep.

★ Earth's temperature allows for liquid water to exist, instead of boiling away like on Venus or being frozen as on Mars. All known life-forms need water.

★ Challenger Deep in the Pacific Ocean is the deepest point in Earth's oceans at 10,924 meters (35,840 feet) deep.

★ The Nile in Africa and the Amazon in South America are the world's two longest rivers. Both are more than 6,600 kilometers (4,100 miles) long.

Land Fast Facts

★ Earth's land, rocks, and minerals are its lithosphere.

★ The 30 percent of Earth's surface that is land is covered in mountains, volcanoes, deserts, ice, and freshwater lakes and rivers.

★ Mount Everest is Earth's highest mountain at 8,848 meters (29,028 feet) tall.

★ Cotahuasi Canyon in southwestern Peru is Earth's deepest canyon. At 3.4 kilometers (2 miles) deep, it is twice as deep as the Grand Canyon.

Life Fast Facts

★ The biosphere is the part of Earth where life exists.

★ Earth is the only planet in our solar system where we know there is life. There has been life on Earth for at least 3.5 billion years of its 4.5-billion-year history.

★ Humans have lived on Earth for about 100,000 to 200,000 years.

★ Life of some sort lives nearly everywhere on Earth—land, water, and air. Even boiling hot springs and frozen lakes are home to tiny life-forms.

★ There may be as many as 100 million different species, or kinds, of living things on Earth. Fewer than 2 million species have been identified and named.

Earth Timeline
of Exploration and Discovery

1519–1522—Ferdinand Magellan's crew is the first to sail around the world.

1543—Copernicus states that Earth is a planet moving around the Sun.

1804–1806—Meriwether Lewis and William Clark explore the northwestern United States.

1824—William Buckland describes the first known dinosaur, *Megalosaurus*.

1825—William H. James designs the first scuba suit to explore underwater.

1831–1836—Charles Darwin travels aboard the ship **HMS** *Beagle* and forms his ideas about evolution.

1909—Robert E. Peary is the first person to reach the North Pole.

1911—Roald Amundsen is the first person to reach the South Pole.

1915—Alfred Wegener states that the continents are moving.

1925—The first map of the Atlantic Ocean floor is made.

1951—The deepest ocean point, Challenger Deep, is discovered.

1953—Edmund Hillary and Tenzing Norgay are the first people to climb the world's tallest mountain, Mount Everest.

1957—*Sputnik I* is the first satellite to orbit Earth.

1960—*Television Infrared Observation Satellite (TIROS)*, the first weather satellite, begins photographing clouds and storms from space.

TIMELINE
★

1961—Yuri Gagarin is first human to orbit Earth.

1968—*Apollo 8* astronauts are the first humans to view and photograph Earth from deep space.

1969—*Apollo 11* astronauts are the first humans to walk on the Moon. They collect moon rocks and return them to Earth.

1972—*Landsat 1* begins satellite series that continuously maps Earth's land, discovering and tracking changes in coastlines, forests, ice caps, and wildfires.

1991—*Upper Atmosphere Research Satellite (UARS)* provides evidence that human-made chemicals are causing the Antarctic ozone hole.

1992—*TOPEX/Poseidon* finds connections between Earth's oceans and climate.

1999—Earth-observing satellite *Terra* begins studying global climate change.

2003—*ICEsat* confirms that global warming is melting more of Earth's polar ice sheets.

2010—*Aquarius* is scheduled to measure sea surface saltiness.

2013—*Global Precipitation Measurement (GPM)* is scheduled to measure snow, rain, and ice.

ASTRONAUTS can see evidence of life from space. Parts of Earth's land surface are green with forests. Where do you see life in this picture?

THE MOON

Our big Moon affects Earth in many ways. The Moon's gravity tugs on Earth's oceans, causing the rise and fall of the tides. The sloshing of oceans from the Moon's pull is also slowing down Earth's spin, making our day longer and pushing the Moon farther away. The Moon's gravity also holds Earth's tilt steady. This makes the seasons regular and the climate more stable. Earth without the Moon would be a very different place.

CHAPTER 2

EARTH AS A PLANET

Like the other seven planets in our solar system, Earth moves through space. Right now it is speeding around the Sun at 107,800 kilometers (67,000 miles) per hour, while also spinning around at jet speed. Earth is the largest of the four solid, rocky, terrestrial planets. (Mercury, Venus, and Mars are the others.) Like Saturn, Neptune, and Mars, Earth tilts slightly as it spins. Because of this tilt, part of Earth leans toward the Sun and part leans away as Earth orbits. This creates the changing seasons of Earth's northern and southern hemispheres.

EARTH is made up of crust, mantle, and core. The crust is the rocky outer covering. The mantle is a layer of hot melted rock. The core is mostly iron and nickel metals. Scientists think the inner core is solid and the outer core is liquid.

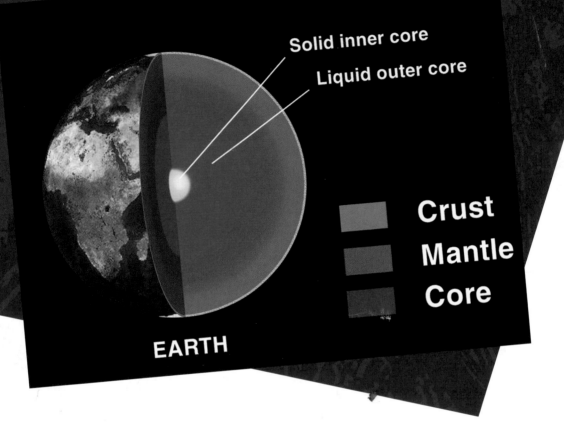

Solid inner core

Liquid outer core

Crust

Mantle

Core

EARTH

OUR ROCKY WORLD

Land covers about 30 percent of Earth's surface. The land's continents and islands are part of the crust, a planet's top rocky layer. On Earth, the crust averages about 40 kilometers (25 miles) thick under land and about 8 kilometers (5 miles) thick under the oceans.

THE Rocky Mountains stretch more than 4,800 kilometers (3,000 miles)— from Canada to New Mexico. This photo shows Rocky Mountain National Park in Colorado (right). Kilauea Volcano erupts in Hawaii (below).

EARTH'S crust is made up of moving plates, shown here in different colors. North America's plate moves west at about as fast as your fingernails grow.

Earth's crust is broken up into huge plates, like pieces of a puzzle. Along the borders of theses plates, a lot happens. Their ramming, spreading, and sliding forces push up mountains, shift continents, and create earthquakes and volcanoes.

28

OUR LIVING, WATERY WORLD

Nearly 70 percent of Earth's surface is covered in oceans at least 4 kilometers (2 ½ miles) deep. Water also runs in rivers, fills up lakes, freezes into ice, and collects underground. Water evaporating into the air becomes clouds that return water to the surface as rain or snow. This ongoing water cycle creates weather and provides fresh water to plants and animals.

Earth is the only planet known to have plants, animals, or life of any kind. Life survives nearly every

FAR-OUT FACT

AH, OXYGEN

Animals, including people, need oxygen to breathe. Earth's atmosphere has some oxygen, but it is mostly nitrogen. Nitrogen gas makes up about 78 percent of our air, oxygen is about 21 percent, and other gases are about one percent. Oxygen is more common in Earth's rocks than its air. About 47 percent of the weight of all rock in Earth's crust is from oxygen. This oxygen is not a gas; it is bound up in the minerals that make up rocks.

place on Earth. Microbes live in boiling hot springs, frozen ice caps, and miles high in the air. Whole ecosystems of sea creatures live in the deep, dark oceans without sunlight. Plants and animals come in many sizes—from too tiny to see, to gigantic whales, to trees taller than buildings that live to be thousands of years old.

GIANT Sequoia trees are some of the largest and longest-living things on Earth. They can grow to 90 meters (300 feet) high and live for 3,000 years.

THIS skull is from the largest and best-preserved *Tyrannosaurus rex* fossil yet discovered. The fossil is named Sue, and it lived on Earth 67 million years ago.

EARTH IS EVER-CHANGING

Life made Earth the planet it is today. Like the other planets, Earth clumped and lumped together out of a cloud of gas and dust. This material was left over when the Sun was born about 4.5 billion years ago. As newborn Earth's center got hotter, the whole planet melted. The heaviest materials, like iron and nickel, sank to the core.

FAR-OUT FACT

ARE THERE OTHER EARTHLIKE WORLDS?

Could Earthlike planets orbit other stars? Maybe. Scientists have discovered hundreds of planets orbiting stars outside our solar system, called exoplanets. One exoplanet discovered in 2007 orbits a star called Gliese 581. It is a rocky world about one-and-a-half times as wide as Earth. This exoplanet also seems to have Earthlike temperatures. Whether or not anything lives on this world or others will take some time to find out. All are too far away to reach by spacecraft.

The lighter minerals floated to the top and became the crust. All this heating and melting also created water, and put gases into the atmosphere.

Young Earth was a very different world. The air had very little oxygen. Earth did not have breathable air until plants started growing. Plants turn carbon dioxide, water, and sunlight into food and oxygen that they give off. This is called photosynthesis. The amount of oxygen in the atmosphere of early Earth increased as plants spread.

Life has existed on Earth for at least 3.5 billion years. We know this from fossils. Some kinds of animals, like dinosaurs, went extinct millions of years ago. Human fossils tell our own short history on this planet. While humanlike fossils as old as 2 million years have been found, modern humans have only been around for 100,000 to 200,000 years. Life is constantly changing—just like our planet.

CHAPTER 3

WHAT'S NEXT FOR EARTH?

Scientists will stay busy tracking our changing planet for years to come. They use many different sorts of orbiting satellites to track global changes happening in oceans, in the atmosphere, and on land. Much of their focus these days is our planet's changing climate. Earth's average temperature is on the rise. This is called global warming. Humans are causing global warming through pollution. Burning fossil fuels, such as gasoline in cars and coal in power plants, adds greenhouse gases to the air, which warms the planet.

Predicting how much our climate will change is difficult—but necessary if we are going to be prepared for the future. Many different things affect climate.

BURNING fossil fuels puts planet-warming greenhouse gases into the air.

The air, ocean, land, and life all affect each other—and the climate. If the ocean warms, sea ice will melt and oceans levels will rise. If a forest is cut down, those trees will no longer take carbon dioxide out of the air.

FAR-OUT FACT

WEATHER VS. CLIMATE

The difference between weather and climate is time. Weather is the conditions of the atmosphere over a short amount of time. Climate is the general weather conditions in an area over a long period of time. For example, Hawaii's climate is warm and tropical. But today's weather in Hawaii might be cool and dry. When scientists talk about climate change, they mean changes in average temperatures and rainfall amounts over many years. So while one hot February day in Chicago does not mean much, warmer average winters over time does mean the climate is changing.

GREENHOUSE GASES AND CLIMATE CHANGE

Like the clear ceiling of a greenhouse, certain gases in the atmosphere trap heat created by warming sunlight. The most abundant of the greenhouse gases is carbon dioxide. Greenhouse gases heat up a planet and cause global warming. While the planet's overall temperature may rise, not all places will necessarily get hotter. A warmer Earth may cause snowier winters in some places and stormier summers in others. That is why some scientists use the more exact term *global climate change* instead of *global warming*.

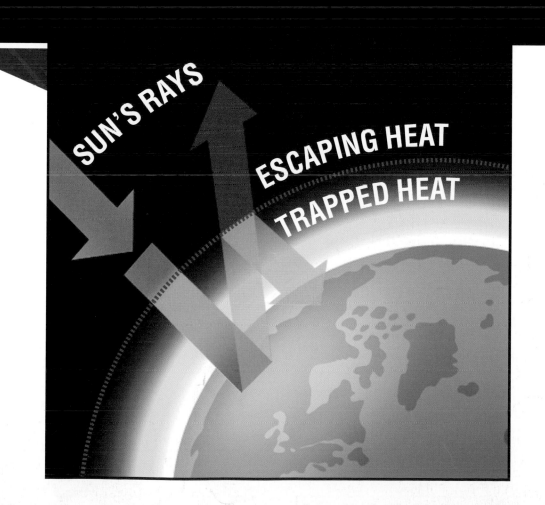

SUN'S RAYS

ESCAPING HEAT

TRAPPED HEAT

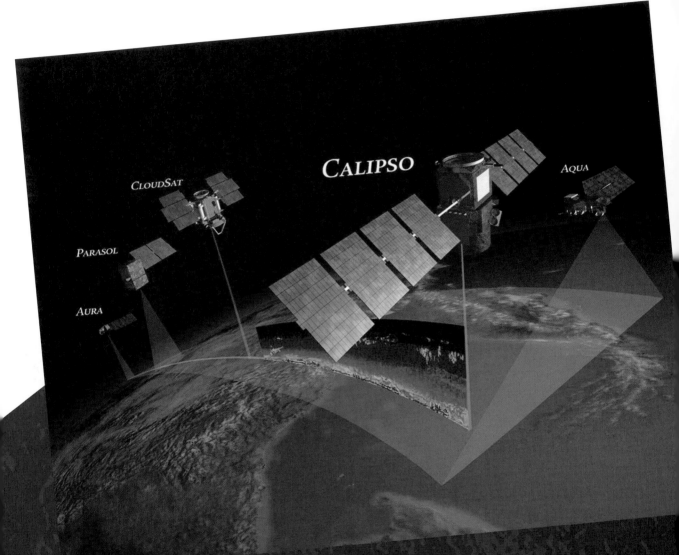

THIS illustration shows the five A-Train satellites that orbit about 705 kilometers (438 miles) above Earth at more than 24,140 kilometers (15,000 miles) per hour. Their names are *Aqua, CloudSat, CALIPSO, PARASOL,* and *Aura.*

ALL ABOARD THE A-TRAIN

One team of Earth-circling satellites working together to track climate change is called the A-Train. The A-Train satellites fly in a formation that takes all five over the same section of Earth one after another within twenty-three minutes. Their overlapping measurements can be compared and shared to find answers to its mission's big question: How is the global Earth system changing?

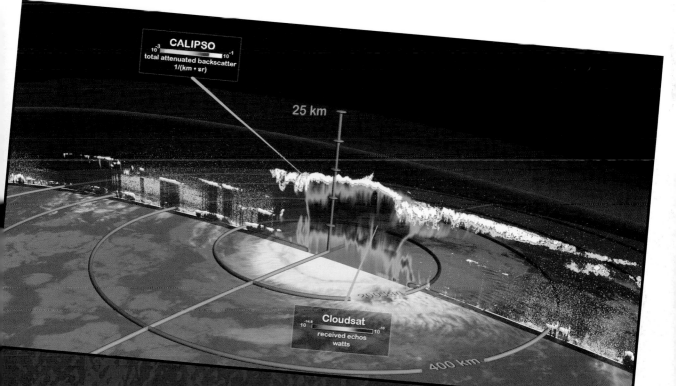

A-TRAIN satellites CloudSat and CALIPSO took these 3-D images of a slice through tropical storm clouds.

FIXING THE OZONE LAYER

In the late 1970s, Earth's ozone layer was becoming thinner. The layer of ozone gas high in Earth's atmosphere protects living things from the Sun's harmful rays. Scientists discovered that chemicals called CFCs were destroying the protective layer. CFCs were used in air conditioners, refrigerators, spray cans, and disposable foam dishes. In 1987, countries around the world banned CFCs. Thanks to the ban, the rate of ozone layer destruction is slowing. But the ozone layer will need another forty years to return to normal.

AURA checks in on Earth's ozone holes. The satellite tracks the ozone layer to see whether the holes are shrinking or growing bigger. This *Aura* image shows Earth's protective ozone layer in green. The blue circle over much of Antarctica is an ozone hole, where the layer is much thinner.

A-Train satellites track clouds, rain, storms, and how the water cycle affects climate. Scientists are learning that clouds can cool land when they block sunlight and create shade. But a thick layer of clouds can also act like a blanket, holding in the day's heat well into the night.

TRACKING AIR POLLUTION

Aura is the A-Train caboose, the last of the six satellites. "*Aura* is offering us a whole new way of looking at how pollution travels around Earth," said Mark Schocberl, the scientist in charge of *Aura*'s mission. Air pollution kills thousands of people each year in the United States alone. Older people, small children, and people with breathing problems, such as asthma, are especially harmed.

Aura discovered that air pollution travels farther than anyone knew. Some of eastern Asia's air pollution floats across the Pacific Ocean all the way to California! Likewise, Europe breathes in some of the pollution that United States factories and vehicles create. "We live in one atmosphere . . . you and I are breathing someone else's exhaust gases," said Schoeberl. Earth's air, like its land and water, are all part of one shared system.

POLAR bears depend on sea ice to get to their hunting grounds.

MORE ON THE WAY

More Earth-observing satellites are on their way—or in the works. Some will measure Earth's gravity or look for earthquakes and volcanoes. Other satellites will continue to track the changes in our planet's climate.

Aquarius is a satellite set to go into Earth orbit in late 2010. Its job will be to measure changes in the saltiness of our oceans. If climate change is melting more sea ice, surrounding oceans will be less salty, like a watered-down drink after the ice cubes have melted. But if warmer ocean water is evaporating more, seawater becomes saltier. *Aquarius* will be able to measure salt changes as small as a pinch of salt in a gallon of water! *Global Precipitation Measurement (GPM)* is another upcoming satellite that will keep an eye on climate change. It is set to launch in 2013. *GPM* will measure rain, snow, and ice around the globe. It will help with weather forecasts, as well as track any changes to Earth's climate over time. Hopefully these and other Earth-observing satellites will help us keep our planet healthy long into the future.

Words to Know

atmosphere—The layer of gases that surrounds a planet, a moon, or another object in space that is held in place by the object's gravity.

biosphere—The region surrounding, on, and within Earth that supports life.

carbon dioxide—A colorless gas that is formed by the burning and breaking down of substances containing carbon.

chlorofluorocarbons (CFCs)—Ozone-layer damaging chemicals in refrigerators, spray cans, and other products that are now mostly banned.

climate—The weather patterns of a place over many years.

climate change—A change in Earth's climate.

diameter—A straight line through the center of a sphere.

environment—All the conditions needed to support life in different forms and the things in the surroundings of a life-form.

evolution—The theory that all living things developed, or evolved, over time from a few simple life-forms.

global warming—The warming of a planet's atmosphere due to greenhouse gases.

gravity—The force of attraction between two or more bodies with mass.

greenhouse gas—A gas that traps heat in an atmosphere, such as carbon dioxide and water vapor.

WORDS TO KNOW

★

hydrosphere—Earth's water, including oceans, lakes, rivers, and water vapor in the air.

lithosphere—Earth's solid land and rock layer.

mass—The amount of matter in something.

meteor—A rock from space that is traveling through an atmosphere; a shooting star.

orbit—The looping or circling path followed by a planet, a moon, or another object in space around another object; to move around an object.

ozone layer—A layer of ozone gas about 48 kilometers (30 miles) above Earth that blocks harmful rays of the Sun.

planet—A large, sphere-shaped object in space that is alone in its orbit around the Sun.

pollution—Human-created harmful substances in the air, water, or land.

precipitation—Rain, snow, or other water that falls from clouds.

satellite—A machine launched into space that orbits Earth.

solar system—A sun and everything that orbits it.

sun—The star in the center of a solar system.

terrestrial planet—A rocky, solid planet with a metal core, such as Mercury, Venus, Earth, and Mars.

volcano—A break in a planet's or moon's surface where melted rock or gas escapes.

volume—The amount of space something fills.

water vapor—Water in gas form.

Find Out More and Get Updates

Books

Bell, Trudy E. *Earth's Journey Through Space.* New York: Chelsea House Publishers, 2007.

Bourgeois, Paulette. *The Jumbo Book of Space.* Toronto: Kids Can Press, 2007.

Carson, Mary Kay. *Exploring the Solar System: A History with 22 Activities.* Chicago: Chicago Review Press, 2008.

Johnston, Andrew K. *Earth From Space.* Tonawanda, N.Y.: Firefly Books, 2007.

Miller, Ron. *Satellites.* Minneapolis, Minn.: Twenty-First Century Books, 2008.

Stille, Darlene R. *Plate Tectonics: Earth's Moving Crust.* Minneapolis, Minn.: Compass Point Books, 2007.

Turner, Pamela S. *Life on Earth—and Beyond: An Astrobiologist's Quest.* Watertown, Mass.: Charlesbridge, 2008.

FIND OUT MORE AND GET UPDATES
★

Solar System Web Sites

You will find lots more information on Earth—and fun space stuff—on these Web sites.

NASA Science for Kids
 <http://nasascience.nasa.gov/kids/earth-science-for-kids>

Solar System Exploration
 <http://solarsystem.nasa.gov/kids>

Earth Exploration Web Sites

Read about Earth observation missions, check out amazing pictures and videos, and learn about climate change.

Earth from Space
 <http://www.earthfromspace.si.edu/>

Earth Observing Satellite Movie
 <http://sci.gallaudet.edu/MSSDScience/a-trainanimation.mpg>

EPA Climate Change Kids Site
 <http://epa.gov/climatechange/kids/>

Landsat
 <http://spaceplace.nasa.gov/en/kids/landsat/>

Index

A

Apollo 8, 9–10
Apollo 11, 10
Arvidson, Terri, 14, 16–17
atmosphere, 6, 7, 29, 33, 34, 36, 37, 40, 41

B

biosphere, 6

E

Earth
distance from Sun, 6
environment, 8
land, 25–26, 28
life, 5, 6, 8, 10, 25, 29–30, 32–33, 34
location, 5
rotation, 5, 24, 25
seasons, 24, 25
size, 5, 25
tilt, 24, 25
water, 6, 8, 9–10, 25, 28–30, 32, 39, 41

Explorer 1, 11

G

global climate change, 36, 39, 43
global warming, 34, 36, 37
gravity, 6, 24, 43

H

hydrosphere, 6

I

International Space Station, 14

L

lithosphere, 6

M

Mars, 6, 25
Mercury, 25
Moon, 9, 10, 24

P

photographs from space, 9, 11–13
pollution, 8, 34, 41

S

satellite, 10–11, 34, 41
Aquarius, 43
A-Train, 36, 39, 41
Global Precipitation Measurement, 43
Landsat, 11–17
Landsat 1, 12
Landsat 5, 17
Landsat 7, 14, 17
Landsat 8, 17
Sputnik, 11
Sun, 5, 6, 7, 25, 32, 40

V

Venus, 6, 25

W

weather, 8, 11, 14, 29, 36, 43

Y

Yellowstone National Park, 12

2 1982 02400 2358